Every
PAUL
Needs a
timothy

Every
PAUL
Needs a
timothy

*Blessings for Teachers
and Small-Group Leaders*

Woodie J. Stevens and J. D. Sailors

BEACON HILL PRESS
OF KANSAS CITY

Copyright 2009
by Woodie J. Stevens, J. D. Sailors, and Beacon Hill Press
of Kansas City

ISBN 978-0-8341-2476-9

Printed in the
United States of America
Cover Art: J. R. Caines
Interior Design: Sharon Page

Library of Congress Cataloging-in-Publication Data

Stevens, Woodie J., 1951-
    Every Paul needs a Timothy : blessings for teachers and small-group leaders / Woodie J.
Stevens and J.D. Sailors.
      p. cm.
    ISBN 978-0-8341-2476-9 (pbk.)
    1. Bible. N.T. Timothy, 1st—Devotional literature. 2. Sunday school teachers—Prayers
and devotions. 3. Church group work—Prayers and devotions. I. Sailors, J. D., 1949-
II. Title.
    BS2745.54.S74 2009
    242'.69—dc22

                                                                        2009023038

10 9 8 7 6 5 4 3 2 1

Contents

God Our Savior

Word for Today

"Paul, an apostle of Christ Jesus by the command of God our Savior and of Christ Jesus our hope, to Timothy my true son in the faith: Grace, mercy and peace from God the Father and Christ Jesus our Lord" (1 Timothy 1:1-2).

Thought for Today

I love the salutation! My letters start with "Dear So-and–So," which lacks any kind of pizzazz at all. Paul starts his letter with more than his own name, but with his vocation given at the command of the divine Godhead. Have you ever thought of God the Father as our Savior? He is. Without His heart of love for the world, we would be totally lost. And it's so good to be reminded of our hope: Christ Jesus. We've put our hope fully on Him and the grace to be given us when He is revealed.

Prayer for Today

Wonderful Counselor, Mighty God, Everlasting Father, Lord God Almighty, Savior of the world, I put my hope and trust in you today. May I take your peace into my warring world and be your agent of love. In your name I pray. Amen.

Stay There

Word for Today

"As I urged you when I went into Macedonia, stay there in Ephesus so that you may command certain men not to teach false doctrines any longer nor to devote themselves to myths and endless genealogies. These promote controversies rather than God's work—which is by faith" (1 Timothy 1:3-4).

Thought for Today

Fear and discouragement sometimes weigh heavily on God's servants. Paul even mentions that he fears he has wasted his efforts on some. Our oft-made solution to discouragement is to say that "I can't do any more for these people" or "The grass must be greener somewhere else." Paul's advice to Timothy is to "stay there." He said it once when they were together, and now he sends the message in this letter—"Stay there." Paul recognizes Timothy's challenges and his opposition but knows that both Timothy and the work will be stronger if Timothy stays put in Ephesus.

Prayer for Today

Eternal Father, may I live this joyful day in the radiant brilliance of your unfailing light. Illuminate my heart, my mind, and my will through your enabling Holy Spirit. Cause me to persevere. Shine in my words and deeds so that your hope, joy, and peace fill each moment and are evident to all. In your Son's name I pray. Amen.

The Channel of Love

Word for Today

"The goal of this command is love, which comes from a pure heart and a good conscience and a sincere faith" (1 Timothy 1:5).

Thought for Today

How does love accomplish its work? It must go through people like you and me. If we're unwilling or unable to let love flow through us, then it simply withers and dies. Love begins in a purified heart. All the poison of unforgiveness and selfishness must be drained before we can love wholeheartedly and without discrimination. Love cannot flow unless we have a good conscience—that is, unless we have no ulterior motives and no hidden agendas in our good deeds. And love cannot reach its recipient unless we are convinced that the power of love is the way God has intended for us to reach and change the hearts of humanity. God is at work loving us and encouraging us to love one another as Christ has loved us.

Prayer for Today

Your Word tells us we were made in your image. But we find our hearts sometimes filled with arrogance and ill will. Would you have compassion on us? Forgive us, and break down the artificial walls of pride, power, and position that separate us. Pierce our heart struggles and confusion with heavenly wisdom and grace so that we may serve you in harmony with those around us through Jesus Christ our Lord. In your name we pray. Amen.

DAY 4

Wannabees

Word for Today

"Some have wandered away from these and turned to meaningless talk. They want to be teachers of the law, but they do not know what they are talking about or what they so confidently affirm" (1 Timothy 1:6-7).

Thought for Today

Those who would be teachers, says James, must know that they will be held to a higher standard (James 3:1). Paul reflects on those whose hearts are less than pure, whose consciences are seared, and whose faith is damaged who still think they want to teach the truths of God. No matter how well they voice their beliefs, how can they understand the things that are only spiritually discerned? How can they teach the truths of the Spirit when they're not in step with the Spirit? Jesus warned against those wolves who, though well-dressed in sheep's clothing, try to teach the things of God. Their teaching is meaningless no matter how dynamic their presentation and how logical their conclusions.

Prayer for Today

Master, confront the arrogant audacity of my independent thinking. Take away my stubborn self-will. Cause me to rely on you for knowledge, understanding, and wisdom and to live in peace today. In your name I pray. Amen.

Meditation on the Law

Word for Today

"We know that the law is good if one uses it properly. We also know that law is made not for the righteous but for law-breakers and rebels, the ungodly and sinful, the unholy and irreligious; for those who kill their fathers or mothers, for murderers, for adulterers and perverts, for slave traders and liars and perjurers—and for whatever else is contrary to the sound doctrine that conforms to the glorious gospel of the blessed God, which he entrusted to me" (1 Timothy 1:8-11).

Thought for Today

What did Paul say? He said that you can't understand the law of God unless you understand the gospel of God. The law judges the actions and attitudes of sinners and those who rebel against God. The law is given to identify and convict those who live outside the realm of God's wonderful grace. No wonder Paul calls the gospel glorious and God himself blessed. Many misuse the law as a standard that supposedly would bring us into a righteous relationship with God. But righteousness is from faith, apart from the works of the law. Post the Ten Commandments anywhere you want, but don't be fooled: they can never save you, only condemn you. Lift Jesus up, as Moses lifted up the snake in the wilderness, so humanity can look and live.

Prayer for Today

Dear Lord, I don't ask for more blessings or more things to consume. I don't ask for some ecstatic spiritual high or an angelic visitation—but I do ask for a pure heart to better serve you and others. In Jesus' name I pray. Amen.

Thank the Lord

Word for Today

"I thank Christ Jesus our Lord, who has given me strength, that he considered me faithful, appointing me to his service" (1 Timothy 1:12).

Thought for Today

The gospel had been given to Paul from the Lord Jesus (Galatians 1:12). But Paul received more than just the words and the message of the Cross and the Resurrection; he received empowerment. Have you seriously thought about what Paul did with his life—the places he went, the miles he covered, the opposition he faced, and the burden for Christ's church that he carried? It's amazing and staggering to believe that one man could have accomplished and endured what he did. Read slowly and thoughtfully 2 Corinthians 11:23-29, and get a snapshot of the life and ministry of Paul. Paul was called, empowered, strengthened, renewed, and confident. He knew his call, his ministry, and his Savior.

Prayer for Today

Dear Lord, I need wisdom to speak right, strength to live right, power to love right. Thank you for being all I need. In your precious name I pray. Amen.

I Was Shown Mercy

Word for Today

"Even though I was once a blasphemer and a persecutor and a violent man, I was shown mercy because I acted in ignorance and unbelief" (1 Timothy 1:13).

Thought for Today

Paul was a living testimony of the transforming power of the gospel of Jesus Christ. What an incredible change happened in his life because of his encounter with Jesus Christ on the road to Damascus! That trip was intended to bring the church of Jesus to an end. Paul was intent on destroying the faith of Jesus' followers. He spoke against Jesus of Nazareth as Messiah. He arrested believers who dared come to the synagogues. He consented to the deaths of Christians, including the martyr Stephen. Paul was convinced that he was defending the name of God and the faith of Israel by what he did. But Christ stopped him in his tracks and revealed himself with the words "Saul, Saul, why do you persecute me?" (Acts 9:4). The merciless man was shown God's full mercy.

Prayer for Today

Merciful Father, how great is your goodness to me! How blessed I am to have fellowship with you! I bless your name forever. May everything you created praise you and recognize that we are dependent upon your generous grace and infinite love. You are amazing and marvelous. In your Son's powerful name I pray. Amen.

Grace Poured Out

Word for Today

"The grace of our Lord was poured out on me abundantly, along with the faith and love that are in Christ Jesus" (1 Timothy 1:14).

Thought for Today

Paul did not just barely make it into the realm of grace. When the Lord's grace was poured out on him, it just kept coming and coming. And Paul declares, "There was more than enough!" He was given what he had lacked as a zealous Jew. He was given everything he had lacked as the persecutor of the Church. He was given faith in Christ Jesus. As the words of the hymn "Amazing Grace" put it, *How precious did that grace appear / The hour I first believed!* Have you considered how marvelous it is to believe in Jesus as the Christ of God? And Paul was given love for all the people he had previously hated so thoroughly. As Peter would say, he had been given everything he needed for life and godliness in this present age (2 Peter 1:3).

Prayer for Today

Dear Lord, I'm filled with wonder at how you work in my life. You're providing, directing, shaping, growing, and loving me. I'm grateful for your presence, which is with me always. In Christ's name I pray. Amen.

Trustworthy Saying

Word for Today

"Here is a trustworthy saying that deserves full acceptance: Christ Jesus came into the world to save sinners—of whom I am the worst" (1 Timothy 1:15).

Thought for Today

Did God make an exception when he saved Saul the persecutor? Did He really intend to convert and restore to himself such a wicked and violent person? The answer is "Absolutely!" Paul's conversion may have been exceptional, but it was not an exception to the intent and the power of the grace of God. God did exactly what He intended to do—save sinners. If we fully accept this trustworthy saying, then we'll never view any sinner without knowing that Christ died for him or her and that God's arm is not so short that He cannot help. Who is it who's so far gone from righteousness and God that you would not have an ounce of faith that God could help him or her? Think again: "Christ Jesus came into the world to save sinners."

Prayer for Today

Help me, O Lord, to have wisdom in my words, clarity in my thoughts, love in my spirit, and passion in my soul, that I might be used today to introduce to you someone you came to save. In Jesus' name I pray. Amen.

Unlimited Patience

Word for Today

"For that very reason I was shown mercy so that in me, the worst of sinners, Christ Jesus might display his unlimited patience as an example for those who would believe on him and receive eternal life" (1 Timothy 1:16).

Thought for Today

Paul introduces us to the concept of the unlimited patience of Christ Jesus. Christ displayed it in Paul for the purpose of letting everyone know that it continues to be available to anyone and everyone. The goal is that we might believe in Jesus as the Christ and receive the gift of eternal life. In John 17:3 eternal life is defined as knowing the one true God and the one He sent on our behalf: Jesus Christ. Paul only thought he knew God before he met Jesus. It was not until he came to know Christ that he ever knew who the only true God was. How long will Christ wait for the sinner to turn to Him? He'll wait as long as it takes (see 2 Peter 3:9).

Prayer for Today

Father, grant me tolerance and patience to wait with wisdom as others are drawn to you through your gracious love and mercy. You're always doing more than we perceive. Be exalted. In your Son's name I pray. Amen.

Sneaking in a Benediction

Word for Today

"Now to the King eternal, immortal, invisible, the only God, be honor and glory for ever and ever. Amen" (1 Timothy 1:17).

Thought for Today

The benediction is not always the last word, but by definition it's always a good word. Paul breaks out in praise at the very thought of what God has done for him in Christ Jesus. Sometimes we all need a trip back down memory lane to recall the blessings that God has given us. And we learn something about God from Paul's adjectives. Number one—He is the King of eternity. That makes Him the first and last Sovereign. He owns it all, He will rule it all, and He will judge it all. He is immortal. That should not surprise us. What does surprise us is that without Him we are not a candidate for life at all, let alone immortality. He is invisible to us. But we're not invisible to Him. He sees us at all times. We see Him only through eyes of faith. He is the one and only God. Beside Him there is no other. There are no lesser gods, there is no god equal to Him, and there is no one greater than He. There is nothing about Him that is inadequate. He is incomparable. He is God now and forever. Give Him the praise due His name.

Prayer for Today

Thank you. Thank you. Thank you. Thank you, source and giver of all blessings and grace. In the name of my Savior I pray. Amen.

Shipwrecked Faith

Word for Today

"Timothy, my son, I give you this instruction in keeping with the prophecies once made about you, so that by following them you may fight the good fight, holding on to faith and a good conscience. Some have rejected these and so have shipwrecked their faith" (1 Timothy 1:18-19).

Thought for Today

Faith is a vessel that God has given us to carry us to our destination. Faith moves us from death to life. Faith carries us on the glassy surface of the calm, cloudless days. Faith helps us prepare when the storm clouds appear on the horizon. Faith helps us hold on when the seas are rough and the wind is relentless. Faith will always keep us if we treat it as the precious vessel that we know it is. But faith can fail if you let go of it. And if you think and act without faith, your conscience will be weakened and become less than reliable. Have you ever seen the remains of a shipwreck? The breakup of faith is not pretty either. If you shipwreck your faith, you might as well forget about making it to your destination or even surviving at all.

Prayer for Today

Lord Jesus, I trust you. I want to trust you more. I'm certain of what I hope for, and I'm confident that your will is being done in me and in this world. I want to please you as I walk this day, not by what I see but according to your trustworthy Word. In Jesus' name I pray. Amen.

Handed Over to Satan?

Word for Today

"Among them are Hymenaeus and Alexander, whom I have handed over to Satan to be taught not to blaspheme" (1 Timothy 1:20).

Thought for Today

Paul does not explain what he means by "handed over to Satan." This is clearly an early practice of church discipline as Jesus had taught the disciples in Matthew 18:17. Paul had already practiced expelling someone from the church as described in 1 Corinthians 5. The hope is that those separated from the fellowship of the church, or from any Christian, would come to their senses and repent of any immoral or ungodly lifestyle. Sin cannot be harbored in the Body of Christ or in the heart of any individual. Shunning is drastic but appropriately necessary at times. There must always be hope of repentance and restoration.

Prayer for Today

Master, your unending love has led me to repentance, and your amazing grace has restored my soul. Now lead me through this day in the hope of the eternal welcome you're preparing for me and for all who love you. In your powerful name I pray. Amen.

For Those in Authority

Word for Today

"I urge, then, first of all, that requests, prayers, intercession and thanksgiving be made for everyone—for kings and all those in authority, that we may live peaceful and quiet lives in all godliness and holiness" (1 Timothy 2:1-2).

Thought for Today

Are you Republican or Democrat? With regard to praying for those in authority, it shouldn't make a difference. You should pray for anyone and everyone who governs, regardless of his or her race, gender, religious beliefs, or political affiliation. That includes intercession for needs, wisdom, and even salvation. In recent times I've observed that Christians in our country spend more time criticizing leadership than praying for them. Not surprisingly, I've also seen that same supercritical attitude turn against pastors and other church leaders. Have we unleashed something we cannot control, and are we reaping what we have sown? If we will be salt and light and pray for those in authority, we will be able to live peaceful and quiet lives in all godliness and holiness.

Prayer for Today

Almighty God, you give and you take; you raise up leaders and take leaders down. You have mercy on whomever you choose to have mercy on and bless with grace those who love you. Fill my heart with peace and hope as I trust in you to direct my steps. In Christ's name I pray. Amen.

Pleasing to God

Word for Today

"This is good, and pleases God our Savior, who wants all men to be saved and to come to a knowledge of the truth" (1 Timothy 2:3-4).

Thought for Today

If someone would tell us one thing that would help us please our God, would we do it? Here it is, and it is way too simple. Why wouldn't we do it all the time? Is it because we're over-absorbed with our own prayer requests? Is it because there are certain people for whom we refuse to pray? Is it because we're too busy complaining about our leadership to pray for them? Look at the verse again. Could it be that our shortcoming in this area is the reason that some are not saved and many will never come to understand the truth of God? Look at John 20:21-23. What has Jesus commanded? If we're not showing and sharing the love and forgiveness of Christ, how will the world ever catch on to the power of forgiveness and the goodness of God?

Prayer for Today

O Lord, your ways are above my ways and Your thoughts far beyond mine. You defend the fatherless, the widow, the poor, and the needy. You care about how we treat each other. You are my friend. Help me be a friend to those you love. In Jesus' name I pray. Amen.

The Basics

Word for Today

"There is one God and one mediator between God and men, the man Christ Jesus, who gave himself as a ransom for all men—the testimony given in its proper time" (1 Timothy 2:5-6).

Thought for Today

There is no need to sit around and wait to see if another God will replace the one we know about. The words "Hear, O Israel: The LORD our God, the LORD is one" are not up for revision. God is God. There is no change there. But He has been busy revealing things about himself that were not known before. He has revealed that He has a Son. He has revealed the one and only mediator who is also the ransom paid for our sins. We may not know everything about God, but what we do know, because He has revealed it to us, is huge. This ransom of himself is inclusive: it is the "ransom for all men." That is why we should be praying for everyone, no matter who he or she may be.

Prayer for Today

Gracious Lord Jesus, I find it amazing that you would die for me, be raised to life for me, and are interceding for me at the right hand of the Father. I cannot fathom that you're willing to live in my heart. It's astounding, incomprehensible that the love of God is shed abroad in my heart! How grateful I am! Blessed be the name of the Lord. In the name of my Savior I pray. Amen.

You're Not Kidding, Are You?

Word for Today

"For this purpose I was appointed a herald and an apostle—I am telling the truth, I am not lying—and a teacher of the true faith to the Gentiles" (1 Timothy 2:7).

Thought for Today

Paul has been telling Timothy to pray for all people, because God has sent Christ as a ransom for all humanity. Now he becomes more specific about whom to pray for. To get the full import of what he's saying, we must understand how painful it was for Jews to think that a Gentile could be saved at all or that Jews would be responsible to take the good news to non-Jews. A reading of Acts 22:21-22 shows what a drastic mind-shift Paul introduced. A complete study of Acts and Galatians shows that Paul paid dearly to fulfill his God-given mission of taking the true faith to the Gentiles. Paul's purpose? To ensure that all humanity would know that Christ died for each of us.

Prayer for Today

I pray for my interactions with each person I meet today. Help me treat everyone with a spirit of peace, acceptance, and love. May others sense in my words and my deeds that you're governing each thought and feeling. May they sense you guiding all my responses to the events of this day. Help them to see that I trust in you alone for my eternal destiny and for the moments of this day. In Christ's name I pray. Amen.

All Men Everywhere

Word for Today

"I want men everywhere to lift up holy hands in prayer, without anger or disputing" (1 Timothy 2:8).

Thought for Today

Please don't disconnect this line of Scripture from what Paul has been teaching. This has nothing to do with posture in prayer and everything to do with unity of attitude toward the lost. Psalm 24 speaks of a man standing before God with clean hands and a pure heart and receiving vindication from his Savior. Jesus taught us to pray, "Your kingdom come, your will be done on earth as it is in heaven." All humanity lifting hands in prayer without anger or disputing would certainly be a sign of the coming of the Kingdom. If they did so while lifting each other's hands, the Kingdom would be here in its fullness!

Prayer for Today

Spirit of the living God, help me help others—when it's easy and when it's hard; when I want to and when I don't. When I can and even when I can't, may I always be sensitive to what your Spirit is saying to my spirit. Then you'll get the credit, honor, and glory. In the name of Jesus I pray. Amen.

Dress for Worship

Word for Today

"I also want women to dress modestly, with decency and propriety, not with braided hair or gold or pearls or expensive clothes, but with good deeds, appropriate for women who profess to worship God" (1 Timothy 2:9-10).

Thought for Today

I'm trying to imagine the cultural setting that Paul is addressing, but frankly I can't! I'm trying to think of the many Christian women I've known over the years and wonder how they would react if I had sent them a letter with this instruction. Excuse me while I laugh and duck. I recall those who were always appropriately dressed: modest outwardly and extremely rich inwardly. As I think of them, I don't remember exactly how they dressed, but I certainly remember their beautiful attitudes and thoughtful actions.

Prayer for Today

Heavenly Father, help me receive this new day as an indescribable gift from you. Help me step into my world with the joy and anticipation that each moment is full of potential to bring honor and praise to your holy name. Sensitize me to the marvelous privileges of daily life, and cause me to delight in the knowledge of your presence ever with me. In Jesus' name I pray. Amen.

DAY 20

With All Due Respect

Word for Today

"A woman should learn in quietness and full submission. I do not permit a woman to teach or to have authority over a man; she must be silent. For Adam was formed first, then Eve" (1 Timothy 2:11-13).

Thought for Today

Let's give Paul some credit for his time: he wanted women to learn! If we look at Paul's relationship to Lydia (Acts 16:14), we see a man who treated women with all due respect. Check out Romans 16, and see the women to whom Paul sends greetings. In Philippians 4:3 he names two women "who have contended at my side in the cause of the gospel." If this Timothy passage was all we had to color our view of women in the Church, we would be stuck. Paul speaks of his general practice in the churches of his day and even gives a reason that sounds slightly scriptural—although most of us would question his logic in this case. Were the women of Ephesus overdressed, undereducated, and always asking questions while their husbands were trying to learn? I don't know. I only know that it may be a possibility. Paul had reasons that fit that time. All I know is that some of the best teaching and preaching I have ever heard have come from women.

Prayer for Today

I surrender all my freedom, my knowledge and understanding. I submit my will, my passion and pride and everything I call mine. I gladly return them all to you, because you gave them all to me. Now take all that's yours, and use it according to your purposes and will. I'm satisfied with your love, joy, and peace. I pray in Jesus' name. Amen.

Long Connection

Word for Today

"Adam was formed first, then Eve. And Adam was not the one deceived; it was the woman who was deceived and became a sinner" (1 Timothy 2:13-14).

Thought for Today

What can we really learn from going back to the creation of man and woman and their fall from innocence? Man was formed first and given the command about the trees in the garden. It would have been his responsibility to teach God's command to his wife. Was it Eve's fault that she was deceived? The short answer must be yes. But a check of Genesis will remind you that Adam was right there with the lady as she ate the forbidden fruit. Should he not have stopped her if he was to be her authority? Paul himself taught that sin came through the first man (Romans 5:12), and death also came through him (1 Corinthians 15:21-22). It is in Adam that we all die, not Eve. If men or women would learn, they would be less likely to be led astray or to lead others away.

Prayer for Today

Sovereign Lord, I'm traveling an uncertain path today. There's so much I don't know about what's around the corner. It's easy for me to be fearful and timid. I ask you to help me at the intersections of my daily conversations. Cause me to speak with gentle kindness and winsome grace. Help those who listen sense your amazing love and goodness to me. Through your Spirit, would you be pleased to speak a quiet word of peace to our weary souls today? I ask this in Jesus' name. Amen.

Focus on Faith

Word for Today

"Women will be saved through childbearing—if they continue in faith, love and holiness with propriety" (1 Timothy 2:15).

Thought for Today

Woman's punishment pronounced at the expulsion from the garden was that she would experience increased pain in childbearing (Genesis 3:16). Yet when her first child was born, Eve credited God for helping her with the birth of her son (Genesis 4:1). Paul uses a word translated here "saved," which could easily mean "protected." As God helped Eve, He graciously protects and watches over the childbearing process for preserving Adam's race. And women are protected—saved, if you prefer—by persistence in faith, love, and holiness, or purity. Paul believes strongly in the possibility of faithful, loving women whom the Lord has set aside expressively for His holy purposes.

Prayer for Today

Heavenly Father, speak to your servant today. Cause me to be sensitive to your gentle whispers and to your strong shakings. Help me hear what your Spirit is saying today and help me boldly share it with someone else. In the name of Jesus I ask this. Amen.

Heart Set on a Noble Task

Word for Today

"Here is a trustworthy saying: If anyone sets his heart on being an overseer, he desires a noble task" (1 Timothy 3:1).

Thought for Today

Paul says that being an overseer in the church is worthwhile work. We have taken the word for "overseer" and rephrased it as "bishop" and "superintendent," while the word carries the connotation of a "visiting inspector for the purpose of relief." How many times does a pastor or worker pray for someone to take some pressure off rather than continually put more pressure on? What could be more noble than wanting to help the church of our Lord Jesus to prosper and flourish? Pray for those who take on the daunting task of overseeing.

Prayer for Today

Father God, I don't understand your ways, but you know mine. You never leave me, but I'm lonely; you're my help, but I feel helpless; you're my peace, but I'm full of fear. Have mercy on me, and restore the joy of my salvation. Renew a right spirit within me, and at the end of this day, whatever it holds, I'll praise your holy name. In your Son's name I pray. Amen.

Above Reproach

Word for Today

"Now the overseer must be above reproach, the husband of but one wife, temperate, self-controlled, respectable, hospitable, able to teach, not given to drunkenness, not violent but gentle, not quarrelsome, not a lover of money" (1 Timothy 3:2-3).

Thought for Today

Who is this leader Paul describes? He or she is a leader under control, a person of principle, a person who cares about other people more than self. He or she is a person with nothing to prove except that he or she delights in being a person of God. This is a person who does not use position for self-glory, gain, or self-aggrandizement. Rather, this is a genuinely decent person who comes to help and encourage the Church and its pastors.

Prayer for Today

Holy Spirit of Jesus, the Christ, counselor and friend, light, life, and consuming fire, fall once again upon your Church. Let your fire fall with a fresh anointing of faith, power, and vision upon the Bride of the Lamb. Fill all pastors, teachers, evangelists, and prophets with enabling power as they lead us according to your holy will. Through the holy name of Jesus we ask. Amen.

Your Family

Word for Today

"He must manage his own family well and see that his children obey him with proper respect. (If anyone does not know how to manage his own family, how can he take care of God's church?)" (1 Timothy 3:4-5).

Thought for Today

Everyone who knows about bishops and superintendents knows that they spend a lot of time away from home. The demands of the position are enormous and grueling. It seems almost impossible for such a person to give the attention to his or her family that's necessary and deserved. With that in mind, every supervisor should be sympathetic to the conditions of pastors and church workers who are called away from the home life way too often. Families need love, and love is spelled *t-i-m-e*. Lost sons and daughters are too big a price to pay for larger churches.

Prayer for Today

Master, you said you would build your church. I've been busy trying to build your church, but that's not my job. My job is to do what you told me to do. Help me focus on the mission—to make disciples. Forgive me for trying to do what you said you would do and for neglecting my responsibility to intentionally pursue the mission of making disciples. In Jesus' name I pray. Amen.

Hold Off a Little While

Word for Today

"He must not be a recent convert, or he may become conceited and fall under the same judgment as the devil" (1 Timothy 3:6).

Thought for Today

Satan, known as angel of light, was thrown out of heaven because of his own overblown sense of self-importance. Paul says, "Those who think they are something when they are nothing deceive themselves." Timothy is warned about being too hasty in approving or appointing persons who have not walked the way of faith for a while. A time of probation is sensible. It serves to remind all of us that facing trials and becoming mature in the faith are necessary if we hope to successfully lead others.

Prayer for Today

Sometimes, Lord, the battle is so intense that I grow weary and disheartened by circumstances that remain unchanged. Lead me to your place of peace. Quiet my mind, and help me stay calm and relaxed as you work in me your will and grace. I'll trust you and give you praise for your faithfulness. In Christ's wonderful name I pray. Amen.

The Devil's Trap

Word for Today

"He must also have a good reputation with outsiders, so that he will not fall into disgrace and into the devil's trap" (1 Timothy 3:7).

Thought for Today

The devil does not set traps for prey he already has. He has already snared plenty of captives. Beware! He knows our weaknesses and works overtime to get us to do anything that will ruin our witness and influence for Christ. We need a transparency of life, motives, and intentions that sets us on a higher plain. Satan will set traps regularly for us to fudge and compromise our highest values. Then he'll work overtime to expose our indiscretions. It's one of his favorite ploys, and he has gotten away with it for years. We may be aware of the devil's schemes, but we must still work hard to avoid them at all costs.

Prayer for Today

Dear Lord, you know my thoughts and my words before I even speak. Guard my mind, and fill my heart with wisdom and truth. Shape my motives to honor you, and cause me to walk in your Spirit. In Jesus' name I pray. Amen.

Sincere

Word for Today

"Deacons, likewise, are to be men worthy of respect, sincere, not indulging in much wine, and not pursuing dishonest gain" (1 Timothy 3:8).

Thought for Today

You may be familiar with the word picture that goes with the word "sincere." It originally meant "without wax." Marble statues sold by merchants could be doctored so that cracks and blemishes in the stone carving were filled in with paraffin to hide the defect. When the statues were set out in the blazing summer sun, the wax would melt away, and all the imperfections would be easily seen. Statues sold as *sincere* were guaranteed to be "without wax" to hide faults—what you see is what you get. But the Greek word Paul uses here has its own word illustration. It is *dilogos*, which means "to say two words at once," or to tell a different story. We might call it being two-faced or talking out of both sides of your mouth. I remember the movie line from the Native American who talked of the settler and the politician's lies: "White-man speak with forked tongue." Are we who we purport ourselves to be?

Prayer for Today

Holy desire of my heart, flow your Spirit through me today. Match my words, motives, thoughts, ambitions, and actions. Enable me to be the same with you as I am with others. In the name of Christ I pray. Amen.

Keep Hold

Word for Today

"They must keep hold of the deep truths of the faith with a clear conscience" (1 Timothy 3:9).

Thought for Today

Are you safe with truth? Or perhaps it should be asked, "Is the truth safe with you?" Is what you believe so deeply embedded in your mind and heart that it can't be perverted or compromised? Do you teach anything someone else has taught you without the confidence that you really believe it yourself? The deep truths of the faith hold us when we hold them:

I know whom I have believed and am persuaded that he is able to keep that which I have committed unto him against that day (*2 Timothy 1:12*).

I am convinced that . . . neither height nor depth, nor anything else in all creation, will be able to separate me from the love of God that is in Christ Jesus our Lord (*Romans 8:38-39*).

By this gospel you are saved, if you hold firmly to the word I preached to you. Otherwise, you have believed in vain (*1 Corinthians 15:2*).

We have come to share in Christ if we hold firmly till the end the confidence we had at first (*Hebrews 3:14*).

Prayer for Today

Sovereign God, I rejoice that I am in your grasp. I can't hold you, but you hold me. I'm grateful. I pray in Jesus' name. Amen.

Test First

Word for Today

"They must first be tested; and then if there is nothing against them, let them serve as deacons" (1 Timothy 3:10).

Thought for Today

Grandma Nabors gave me a little ceramic Native American with a cockeyed headband and a little lasso attached to a note that read, "Good Indians test their ropes first!" It was a get-well gift and a little reminder following a church fishing trip in the Gulf of Mexico off Corpus Christi, Texas, with some men from our church.

"Pastor, you go up first! Grab the rope and pull yourself onto the platform."

The platform was an unmanned oil derrick about three miles off Padre Island. My feet made it to the platform, and I was about forty-five degrees from making it when the rope broke. I did the "Nestea plunge" back into the small boat that had brought us out into the Gulf. I heard "crack, crack, crack" as my ribs met Bud's knees and my elbow exploded into his forearm.

Giving folks authority without testing their character and knowing their weaknesses often results in tragedies that no one cares to brag about.

Prayer for Today

I want to run today, O Lord, and not be weary. I want to walk and not faint. So I'm waiting for you. Come close to me as I come close to you. Renew me now with your Spirit. I pray in Christ's name. Amen.

DAY 31

Personal Conduct

Word for Today

"Although I hope to come to you soon, I am writing you these instructions so that, if I am delayed, you will know how people ought to conduct themselves in God's household, which is the church of the living God, the pillar and foundation of the truth" (1 Timothy 3:14-15).

Thought for Today

It matters how we act, and it matters how we treat each other. Paul has written to Timothy about worship and especially in regard to qualifications for church leaders. The Church is and should be "the pillar and foundation of the truth." We ought to be doing righteousness. And when we consider making exceptions, it shouldn't be because the truth doesn't matter and the standards aren't important, but because we choose to show grace to those who have been deeply affected by our fallen world.

Prayer for Today

Merciful Father God, I confess I do not know or understand the throbbing anxieties of those you have called me to serve. But you care for them as sheep without a shepherd. Give me a fresh anointing of patience and kindness and a spirit of humility, that I might serve you by serving the needs of others. In the name of your Son I pray. Amen.

Some Will Abandon the Faith

Word for Today

"The Spirit clearly says that in later times some will abandon the faith and follow deceiving spirits and things taught by demons" (1 Timothy 4:1).

Thought for Today

We have to pay attention to this. If we teach, we must hear it. If we're being taught by anyone, we must be fully aware of what the Spirit has clearly said about these later times. Can everything being taught in the name of Jesus be true? We want it to be, but it simply isn't. Have you ever watched someone who has been brainwashed by an eccentric idea—thinking it must be true just because he or she thought it? The gospel is simple and doesn't need goofy quirks to make it more exciting. Paul gives the demons credit for swaying people to teach misleading concepts.

Prayer for Today

Father God, set me free from selfish pride and arrogance. Cause me to think right of myself and of you. Remind me often of your eternal laws and eternal love. Help me look at the issues of today from your eternal perspective. In Jesus' name I pray. Amen.

Seared

Word for Today

"Such teachings come through hypocritical liars, whose consciences have been seared as with a hot iron" (1 Timothy 4:2).

Thought for Today

Preachers, evangelists, and teachers, beware of the sound of your own voice! If you can say something that you've convinced yourself is right but say it so well that anyone at all believes what you've said is from God, you're treading where you ought never to go. Jesus talked about it being better to have a millstone draped over your head and neck and be thrown into the sea than to cause one of His little ones to stumble. Be grounded in the Word. If your teaching comes from anywhere else—drop it as unnecessary or dangerous or both. This Word teaches that if we are preaching the truth and not living up to the truth, we've disqualified ourselves from the prize.

Prayer for Today

Dear Lord Jesus, help me keep my heart warm with love and devotion. Break up the hard spots in my soul, and remove the stones of doubt. Root out any stubborn thorns of self-sufficiency and pride. Cultivate and fertilize my spirit with your Word, wisdom, and ways. In Christ's name I pray. Amen.

Control Freaks

Word for Today

"They forbid people to marry and order them to abstain from certain foods, which God created to be received with thanksgiving by those who believe and who know the truth. For everything God created is good, and nothing is to be rejected if it is received with thanksgiving, because it is consecrated by the word of God and prayer" (1 Timothy 4:3-5).

Thought for Today

If you believed as the gnostics did, that the present material world was evil, then it might make sense to abstain from everything you could: marriage, relationships, and foods that are not the basic necessities. If you believed what they believed, it would be unavoidable to sin every day in thought, word, and deed. But we believe that everything God created is good, including marriage and a wonderful variety of foods. Gnostics had people afraid of everything in this world. Christians know to "test everything and hold on to the good" (1 Thessalonians 5:21).

Prayer for Today

Lord and Master, through the varied moments of this day, remind me this world is not my home. I'm a citizen of your kingdom. I rejoice in all you've made. I celebrate your watch-care and provision. Keep me from undue concerns, and cause me to walk in faithful obedience and trust. Then you will be glorified, and you will receive praise. In Jesus' name I pray. Amen.

A Good Minister

Word for Today

"If you point these things out to the brothers, you will be a good minister of Christ Jesus, brought up in the truths of the faith and of the good teaching that you have followed" (1 Timothy 4:6).

Thought for Today

Paul is teaching Timothy that there is a time to refute error but also a time to teach the truths of the faith. You don't have to be against everything to be for something. We're to focus principally on *what we are for*. If we explain it well enough, error will be exposed. But Paul is clear that Timothy has done more than just believing and teaching the truth—he has been a follower of it as well. How refreshing to have a leader who teaches the cleansing power of Jesus and lives it out for everyone to see! Timothy was a good minister of Christ Jesus.

Prayer for Today

Dear Lord, I need you to stir up in me the gift of discernment so I can see the direction I should go. I need your strength, courage, and wisdom to choose the right response at the right time for the right reasons. Thank you for your comforting peace that goes with me now into the rigors and demands of this day. I pray in Jesus' name. Amen.

DAY 36

Deserves Full Acceptance

Word for Today

"This is a trustworthy saying that deserves full acceptance (and for this we labor and strive), that we have put our hope in the living God, who is the Savior of all men, and especially of those who believe" (Timothy 4:9-10).

Thought for Today

Exactly what is Paul saying? He's pointing out to us that he believes strongly that it's imperative that people grasp and cling to the word of life that he's holding out for everyone. It is trustworthy—it is beyond all dispute. Its truths are timely and eternal. And it deserves more than a passing thought or a mere mental assent. The gospel of Jesus Christ is of such great merit that it deserves considered study and assimilation into our lives. It should be unmistakable to everyone who sees us and knows us that we have placed our hope in the God of life.

Prayer for Today

Creator God of all existence, fill me with gratitude for the mega-universes you have made. Thank you for creating us in your own image. Thank you for becoming a human. Thank you for providing reconciliation through Jesus Christ. Thank you for calling me your dearly loved child. Cause me to live the way you would have me live. I pray this in Christ's name. Amen.

Set an Example

Word for Today

"Command and teach these things. Don't let anyone look down on you because you are young, but set an example for the believers in speech, in life, in love, in faith and in purity" (l Timothy 4:11-12).

Thought for Today

Paul wants Timothy to realize that his young age will be a problem to his hearers only if his character and actions become a distraction to his teachings and testimony. Solomon had instructed us to "Remember your Creator in the days of your youth." There is nothing better than to get a good start on faith and purity. The word Paul uses for love is *agape*—the selfless, generous, forgiving type of love. As long as Timothy's life and ministry measure up to what he's teaching, no one should have any problem with his lack of experience in leading the Church of God.

Prayer for Today

Set me free, Lord Jesus, from concern about how others see me. Help me see others as you see them. Cause me to love as you love. I ask this in your name. Amen.

Devote Yourself

Word for Today

"Until I come, devote yourself to the public reading of Scripture, to preaching and to teaching" (1 Timothy 4:13).

Thought for Today

Timothy has a calling and a commission to a ministry of the Word of God. What higher calling can there be? I can't imagine handling and dispensing anything of more value. Remember that in that day there were limited copies of the Scripture—the Old Testament—and only a minority of the people had access. Public reading may have been their only chance to hear. Timothy was to expound on what he read by preaching and teaching the truth. Unless a teacher's or preacher's devotion is to minister the Word, he or she has surrendered to something of much less eternal value.

Prayer for Today

Living Word of God, saturate me with the light of your truth. Light of life, penetrate to the depths of my being, and drive out all darkness from my mind, will, and emotions. Fill me with your radiating love so that everyone I meet today might know you through me. I pray in the name of Jesus. Amen.

The Gift

Word for Today

"Do not neglect your gift, which was given you through a prophetic message when the body of elders laid their hands on you" (1 Timothy 4:14).

Thought for Today

What was Timothy's gift? We're not told exactly, but we would not be too far off track to guess that it might have been preaching and teaching. Whatever it was, it was not to be neglected in its use and development. It's been often said, "A call to preach is a call to prepare." At some point that may mean college, Bible college, or seminary. But even past formal education, the gift cannot be neglected. May I be so bold as to say that a call to teach is a call to prepare. Teaching and preaching call for continuous learning and personal deepening in the things of the faith.

Prayer for Today

O Lord, my God, grant me understanding that I might know you. Give me diligence to seek you and wisdom to find you. Cause me to live faithfully before you in order that I might help someone else follow you more closely. In Jesus' name I pray. Amen.

Others Are Watching You Grow

Word for Today

"Be diligent in these matters; give yourself wholly to them, so that everyone may see your progress" (1 Timothy 4:15).

Thought for Today

Young Timothy had been left in Ephesus to pastor the church of Jesus Christ. Paul had learned or been concerned that Timothy was being timid and not using the gifts God had given him to their fullest advantage. He was young in a time and place where being young was not always prized or revered. To fulfill his calling and not fall into a pattern that would shortchange his ministry for the rest of his life, Paul was encouraging him to step up to the plate and give it his best effort. What would the church see? They would see his progress. Our first efforts are not always perfect. But we learn from our mistakes, and we refine our skills with use. Like Timothy, we'll get better if we start using our gifts.

Prayer for Today

Dear Lord, lead me to someone sad, and help me give comfort. Show me someone tired, and help me be a refreshing voice. Sensitize me to those who are lonely, and help me cheer them. Use me to strengthen the tempted, guide the perplexed, and double the joy of the happy. Help me do these things in the name of Jesus, because you have done the same for me. I pray in your name. Amen.

Those Who Endure to the End Shall Be Saved

Word for Today

"Watch your life and doctrine closely. Persevere in them, because if you do, you will save both yourself and your hearers" (1 Timothy 4:16).

Thought for Today

Paul encourages Timothy in the ministry of the Word. He summarizes the prodding and goading with an admonition to preach what he lives and live what he preaches. What his hearers need is a long-term example of faithfulness to the things and the ways of God. Holiness is not a snapshot—it is a video without end. Godliness is not a hundred-meter dash—it is a marathon. What good teachers teach and how they live affect themselves and, thankfully, so many others as well.

Prayer for Today

Today, dear Lord Jesus, I choose to live in your compassion, acceptance, love, forgiveness, and understanding. I choose to share it with those you bring to me. I pray that I will not be discouraged with difficult circumstances but that you will keep my eyes fixed on the issues that are eternally significant. In your name I pray. Amen.

The Family of God

Word for Today

"Do not rebuke an older man harshly, but exhort him as if he were your father. Treat younger men as brothers, older women as mothers, and younger women as sisters, with absolute purity" (1 Timothy 5:1-2).

Thought for Today

There's no one in the Church who is not a member of your family. Jesus taught us to pray, "Our Father . . . give *us* . . . forgive *us* . . . lead *us* not into temptation." Paul will say elsewhere, "None of *us* live to ourselves alone." So Timothy is being taught to leave harshness at the door and treat each person with the utmost respect, because these are the people with whom you live! Be judicious with your words. Once said, they cannot be taken back.

Prayer for Today

Heavenly Father, today I'll be speaking to all kinds of people. I'll be listening to them and responding to them. I'll be asking questions, making comments, telling stories, giving analysis, or even issuing challenges. Help me touch each life through the quickening power of your Spirit. Let the words I say build them up, bless them, and cause them to walk away having benefited from the conversation. In Jesus' name I pray. Amen.

Widows—Part 1

Word for Today

"Give proper recognition to those widows who are really in need. But if a widow has children or grandchildren, these should learn first of all to put their religion into practice by caring for their own family and so repaying their parents and grandparents, for this is pleasing to God" (1 Timothy 5:3-4).

Thought for Today

During the early days of the church back in Jerusalem, the first dispute among believers was over the care of widows. Paul is making it clear to Timothy in today's scripture that it is not the church's responsibility to care for widows if the widow has family to care for her. Widows were vulnerable because there was no welfare system and few employment opportunities for women. It is pleasing to God if children and grandchildren care for their aging parents. (I hope my sons are reading this!) Sometimes the best way a church can help in this is by pointing out the truth to those who should be responsible.

Prayer for Today

Sovereign Lord of all existence, cause the young to rejoice in anticipation of an adventure-filled life serving you. Cause those who are not so young to rejoice in anticipation of immortality and an adventure-filled eternity exploring the amazing wonders of an Almighty God. In Christ's name I pray. Amen.

Widows—Part 2

Word for Today

"Give the people these instructions, too, so that no one may be open to blame. If anyone does not provide for his relatives, and especially for his immediate family, he has denied the faith and is worse than an unbeliever" (1 Timothy 5:7-8).

Thought for Today

Timothy was not to bear this burden alone but to give clear instruction to the believers. A congregation can become overwhelmed and drown in caring for the poor. The first line of defense should always be the family. Paul says that a family who does not care for their own is pagan. This is abandonment at its worst. Men and women who do not care for the elderly in their own families will someday face abandonment by their own descendants because of the pattern they've set in motion.

Prayer for Today

I praise your holy name, Lord Jesus. There's not a day that goes by that you're not with me. Everything I do is known by you. Help me live in the awareness of your constant presence. Grant me wisdom to make right decisions and choices that honor you. Keep me from doing anything that would grieve your Spirit or quench the fires of devotion to you. In your name I pray. Amen.

The Summary

Word for Today

"If any woman who is a believer has widows in her family, she should help them and not let the church be burdened with them, so that the church can help those widows who are really in need" (1 Timothy 5:16).

Thought for Today

Paul has had a lot to say about the care of the widows by and in the church, but he sums up everything he was trying to say with the one sentence of 1 Timothy 5:16. Although we would feel guilty to say that any person was a burden to the church, Paul helps us by saying that some could be. Does that mean we should not help them? No. But if families can be the first line of defense, they should be so to free up the resources of the church to help those who have no other recourse.

Prayer for Today

Father, don't let me be a part of the crowd that stands around complaining and arguing. It's too easy to criticize and quibble over issues of little eternal significance. Help me, Lord, to follow you more closely as I listen, learn, and love. In Jesus' name I pray. Amen.

You'll Never Be Paid
What You're Worth

Word for Today

"The elders who direct the affairs of the church well are worthy of double honor, especially those whose work is preaching and teaching" (1 Timothy 5:17).

Thought for Today

It's an important vocation. Those who do it well are worth far more than they can ever be compensated monetarily. Directing the affairs of the church is a big job, and preaching and teaching only increase the workload. They also increase the value of the servant of God to the church. So how much do you pay a person like that? Paul may be saying that such a person should receive a double paycheck compared to the normal day's pay. Or he might just be saying, "Whatever you're paid, you're worth twice as much as you're receiving!"

Prayer for Today

Gracious Father, in you I've found all that I need and so much more. You've filled me with a marvelous, inexplicable peace and joy. I've found satisfaction in surrender. I've discovered gladness in yielding. I've experienced delight in trusting. I know victory in my soul through the triumphant name of Jesus. I rejoice with profound gratitude to my Savior and Lord. In Jesus' name I pray. Amen.

Accusations

Word for Today

"Do not entertain an accusation against an elder unless it is brought by two or three witnesses. Those who sin are to be rebuked publicly, so that the others may take warning" (1 Timothy 5:19-20).

Thought for Today

The wisdom of the Mosaic Law was that no person could be called to account without the testimony of two or three witnesses. That principle has been carried over to the Church. Timothy said they should not even entertain an accusation—especially against a church leader—unless there are two or more witnesses. That's entirely different from the usual situation of one person accusing and two people believing the accusation. But if anything is proven true, then those leaders should face a public rebuke. We must protect our leaders from lies, but we must also protect the flock from wolves in sheep's clothing.

Prayer for Today

Dear Master of my heart, shine truth upon all my paths so that I won't drift from your calling or wander from your ways. Drive away darkness, pretensions, falsehoods, and selfishness; keep them far from me. Cause me to walk in the integrity of your Word on a clear and clean path of obedience. In Jesus' name I pray. Amen.

Impartiality

Word for Today

"I charge you, in the sight of God and Christ Jesus and the elect angels, to keep these instructions without partiality, and to do nothing out of favoritism" (1 Timothy 5:21).

Thought for Today

The seriousness of the instruction in today's scripture is revealed in the charge that Paul gives to Timothy. God is watching, Jesus Christ is watching, and even the holy angels of God are watching what we say and do. With regard to entertaining accusations against church leaders and rebuking some of the deserving elders, we must not be guilty of rescuing our friends and frying our enemies. Whenever it comes to discipline in the church, we certainly must do to others as we would want them to do to us. When making tough decisions, pray that the shoe will never be on the other foot, but know that it indeed could be.

Prayer for Today

Father, I am weak, but you are strong. Today enable my helplessness with your strength. Enlighten my ignorance with your wisdom. Cleanse my heart with your Word. Fill my emptiness with your love and grace. To the glory of God I pray in Jesus' name. Amen.

The World's Most Famous Instruction

Word for Today

"Stop drinking only water, and use a little wine because of your stomach and your frequent illnesses" (1 Timothy 5:23).

Thought for Today

There are not enough fingers and toes in the world to count the number of times this scripture has been cited to justify drinking alcoholic beverages! But if we look carefully, we get the picture of a young minister who, rather than drinking wine and thus setting a poor example to his flock, was content to drink the water that only further upset his digestive system. We see clearly a young man who apparently had been sick off and on for some time. "Use a little wine," says Paul. Those eager to find a scripture to justify their drinking most often forget that Paul instructed a *little* wine. If Paul had been able to see down through the years what people would do with this personal advice to Timothy, he might have rephrased this instruction!

Prayer for Today

Today, O Lord, I will think, walk, talk, and act. I'll be busy spending my twenty-four hours in all kinds of different activities. Would you be pleased to breathe on me so that my thoughts, work, interactions, and moments are holy and pleasing in your sight? I pray these things in Jesus' name. Amen.

Back to the Subject at Hand

Word for Today

"The sins of some men are obvious, reaching the place of judgment ahead of them; the sins of others trail behind them. In the same way, good deeds are obvious, and even those that are not cannot be hidden" (1 Timothy 5:24-25).

Thought for Today

Paul had interrupted his own train of thought with his personal instruction to Timothy about his illnesses but returns to the instructions about ordaining and commissioning people for ministry. The reason you should not be hasty in the laying-on of hands is that you don't learn everything about a person in just a meeting or two. Some people, eager to become leaders, are very selective in revealing pertinent information that would affect an original decision. Only later will the facts come out that would show the person to be less than forthcoming and certainly unrepentant about untoward circumstances in his or her life. Paul, then, takes a more positive view to realize that a modest person would also fail to fully disclose gracious acts. But the truth will come out, whether good or evil.

Prayer for Today

Lord Jesus, I want to honor you today by how I live. Give me a fresh boldness to face every challenge with a song in my heart, a smile on my face, and a Christlike attitude in my mind. In your wonderful name I pray. Amen.

Under the Yoke of Slavery

Word for Today

"All who are under the yoke of slavery should consider their masters worthy of full respect, so that God's name and our teaching may not be slandered. Those who have believing masters are not to show less respect for them because they are brothers. Instead, they are to serve them even better, because those who benefit from their service are believers, and dear to them. These are the things you are to teach and urge on them" (1 Timothy 6:1-2).

Thought for Today

Thank God that the civilized world is finally free of the scourge of human slavery! We would be appalled if it were ever to be reinstituted among us. Perhaps the other wrongs that the world protects with its laws and customs will also be done away with in coming days. May it be soon that we turn the corner on abortion and child labor and be abhorred that we once sanctioned any of it at all. God's Word never sanctioned slavery—it only gave instructions to slaves and masters who had turned to Christ. We can use these same principles to know how to redeem employee-and-employer relationships. If our actions are truly Christlike, we will enlighten a watching world.

Prayer for Today

Master, I loath this bent toward self-centeredness and pride that's anything but Christlike. Deliver me from considering my interests without including the needs and interests of others. Fill me with the joy of putting Jesus first, me last, and others in between. In your name I pray. Amen.

Conceited False Teachers

Word for Today

"If anyone teaches false doctrines and does not agree to the sound instruction of our Lord Jesus Christ and to godly teaching, he is conceited and understands nothing. He has an unhealthy interest in controversies and quarrels about words that result in envy, strife, malicious talk, evil suspicions and constant friction between men of corrupt mind, who have been robbed of the truth and who think that godliness is a means to financial gain" (1 Timothy 6:3-5).

Thought for Today

Conceit—thinking you know something when you don't—is dangerous and damning. Teaching that promotes controversy stirs up unhealthy factions and leads people astray. False teachers rob people of the truth, because they themselves have been robbed of the truth. This "godliness" that Paul speaks of is only a form and not a reality. Those who oppose Jesus' teaching and see opportunity for financial profit by their own "gospel" are the most disgusting people of all. They have been around from the beginning, and it looks as if they'll continue until Jesus comes.

Prayer for Today

Spirit of God, I open myself entirely for your cleansing, purifying, presence, and power. Strengthen my weaknesses, reveal my hidden faults, empower my witness, and glorify your name. In Christ's name I pray. Amen.

Foolish and Harmful Desires

Word for Today

"People who want to get rich fall into temptation and a trap and into many foolish and harmful desires that plunge men into ruin and destruction. For the love of money is a root of all kinds of evil. Some people, eager for money, have wandered from the faith and pierced themselves with many griefs" (1 Timothy 6:9-10).

Thought for Today

Raise your hand if you would like to get rich! I have to raise mine. I have a great desire to be self-sufficient and owe no one anything. And there are things I would like to have and would like to do. I've latched on to Ecclesiastes 10:19, which tells me, "Money is the answer for everything." In fact, it may be my life verse. But God's Word is clear that as I follow this kind of thinking, I set myself up for temptation and destruction. This love of money, if followed, will eventually take me away from the faith and cause me manifold sorrow. Jesus was right: we cannot serve both God and money.

Prayer for Today

Dear Heavenly Father, I surrender all. I am yours. Do with me as you please. I desire nothing but your will be done in me. I trust in you. I pray in the matchless name of Jesus. Amen.

God's Own Time

Word for Today

"In the sight of God, who gives life to everything, and of Christ Jesus, who while testifying before Pontius Pilate made the good confession, I charge you to keep this command without spot or blame until the appearing of our Lord Jesus Christ, which God will bring about in his own time—God, the blessed and only Ruler, the King of kings and Lord of lords, who alone is immortal and who lives in unapproachable light, whom no one has seen or can see. To him be honor and might forever. Amen" (1 Timothy 6:13-16).

Thought for Today

How long was Timothy to obey Paul's instructions? The answer is easy enough: until Jesus comes. And when will that happen? It will happen in God's own time. And speaking of God, Paul breaks out into a doxology extolling the greatness and awesomeness of this one who gives life to everything! Who is God? Pick it out of Paul's description one phrase at a time, and think about the great truths expressed. See if you can keep from saying with Paul, as he is lost in wonder, love, and praise, one great big "Amen!"

Prayer for Today

Holy, holy, holy. Who am I that your unapproachable light should shine on me? I sing with Isaiah, "Woe to me! I am ruined! For I am a man of unclean lips, and I live among a people of unclean lips, and my eyes have seen the King, the LORD Almighty." Touch my lips, and make them clean. Touch my heart, and make it pure. Touch my life, and fill it completely with your joy. In Jesus' name I pray. Amen.

Lay Up Treasures

Word for Today

"Command those who are rich in this present world not to be arrogant nor to put their hope in wealth, which is so uncertain, but to put their hope in God, who richly provides us with everything for our enjoyment. Command them to do good, to be rich in good deeds, and to be generous and willing to share. In this way they will lay up treasure for themselves as a firm foundation for the coming age, so that they may take hold of the life that is truly life" (1 Timothy 6:17-19).

Thought for Today

Who are the rich people of the world? Most of us define the rich simply as those who have more money than we do. If that's the case, then others have defined us as rich—because clearly we have more than they do! Whatever we have, note this: God has provided it for our enjoyment. But don't miss the joy of being rich in good deeds and the joy of being generous and sharing with others. It's the way we lay up treasure for the coming age. Otherwise there is no foundation!

Prayer for Today

Sovereign Master of all, you've given so much to me. Everything I have comes from your mighty hand of provision. I need one more thing: a grateful heart, not just when I'm pleased and have no pressing need, but always. Constantly fill my heart with praise and blessings, no matter the circumstances. May gratitude be the fountain from which flows my every day. In Christ's name I pray. Amen.

Entrusted to Your Care

Word for Today

"Timothy, guard what has been entrusted to your care. Turn away from godless chatter and the opposing ideas of what is falsely called knowledge, which some have professed and in so doing have wandered from the faith. Grace be with you" (1 Timothy 6:20-21).

Thought for Today

Do we recognize the great value of what we have been given in Christ? Our salvation was bought with the precious blood of Christ. Peter says that it's of greater worth than gold. Those you are mentoring in the faith have been entrusted to your care: God values them so highly that if you cause any of these little ones to stumble, it would be better for you to have a millstone hung around your neck and to be tossed into the deep sea. This gospel is treasure given to us to share—it is the power of God for salvation of everyone who believes. We must not let it be neglected or corrupted. Paul feared for Timothy that somehow he might be led astray. And we should guard ourselves lest we drift from such a great salvation.

Prayer for Today

Spirit of God, set my heart on fire with love. Fill my mind with a passion for holiness. Set my will for selfless action. Move my hands and feet in devoted service for your glory and the benefit of others. In the name of Christ I pray. Amen.